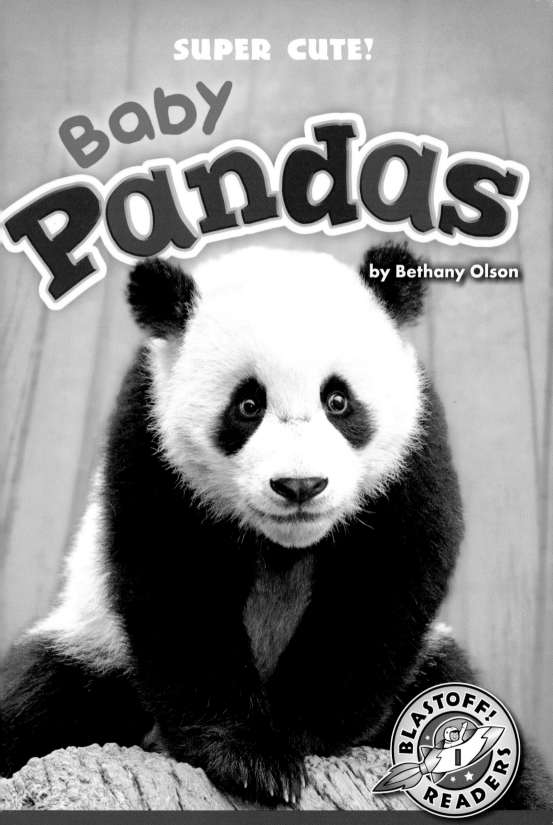

SUPER CUTE!

Baby Pandas

by Bethany Olson

BLASTOFF! READERS

BELLWETHER MEDIA • MINNEAPOLIS, MN

Note to Librarians, Teachers, and Parents:

Blastoff! Readers are carefully developed by literacy experts and combine standards-based content with developmentally appropriate text.

Level 1 provides the most support through repetition of high-frequency words, light text, predictable sentence patterns, and strong visual support.

Level 2 offers early readers a bit more challenge through varied simple sentences, increased text load, and less repetition of high-frequency words.

Level 3 advances early-fluent readers toward fluency through increased text and concept load, less reliance on visuals, longer sentences, and more literary language.

Level 4 builds reading stamina by providing more text per page, increased use of punctuation, greater variation in sentence patterns, and increasingly challenging vocabulary.

Level 5 encourages children to move from "learning to read" to "reading to learn" by providing even more text, varied writing styles, and less familiar topics.

Whichever book is right for your reader, Blastoff! Readers are the perfect books to build confidence and encourage a love of reading that will last a lifetime!

This edition first published in 2014 by Bellwether Media, Inc.

No part of this publication may be reproduced in whole or in part without written permission of the publisher. For information regarding permission, write to Bellwether Media, Inc., Attention: Permissions Department, 5357 Penn Avenue South, Minneapolis, MN 55419.

Library of Congress Cataloging-in-Publication Data

Olson, Bethany.
  Baby pandas / by Bethany Olson.
    p. cm. – (Blastoff! readers. Super cute!)
  Audience: K to grade 3.
  Summary: "Developed by literacy experts for students in kindergarten through grade three, this book introduces baby pandas to young readers through leveled text and related photos"– Provided by publisher.
  Includes bibliographical references and index.
  ISBN 978-1-60014-930-6 (hardcover : alk. paper)
  1. Pandas–Infancy–Juvenile literature. I. Title.
  QL795.P18O47 2014
  599.789'139–dc23
                                                                  2013003495

Printed in the United States of America, North Mankato, MN.

Table of Contents

Panda Cub!

A baby panda
is called a cub.

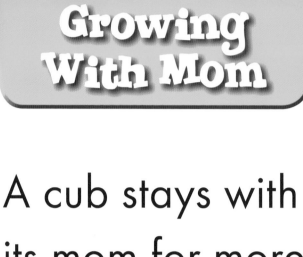

Growing With Mom

A cub stays with its mom for more than a year.

Mom holds her baby close. The cub likes to cuddle.

Mom licks her cub to **groom** it. This also helps them **bond**.

The cub **bleats** when it is hungry. It sounds like a little lamb.

The cub **nurses** when it is young. Later it eats **bamboo**.

bamboo

Time to Move

The cub follows
mom everywhere.
It tries to be just
like her.

The cub climbs trees. It naps on the branches.

The cub rolls around on the ground. That looks like fun!

Glossary

bamboo—a plant with a hard stem that looks like a pole

bleats—makes a noise that sounds like a shaky cry

bond—to become close

groom—to clean

nurses—drinks mom's milk

To Learn More

AT THE LIBRARY

Markle, Sandra. *How Many Baby Pandas?* New York, N.Y.: Walker & Co., 2009.

Schreiber, Anne. *Pandas.* Washington, D.C.: National Geographic, 2010.

Schuetz, Kari. *Giant Pandas.* Minneapolis, Minn.: Bellwether Media, 2012.

ON THE WEB

Learning more about pandas is as easy as 1, 2, 3.

1. Go to www.factsurfer.com.

2. Enter "pandas" into the search box.

3. Click the "Surf" button and you will see a list of related Web sites.

With factsurfer.com, finding more information is just a click away.

Index